Ancient
ROMAN ART

Susie Hodge

Heinemann Interactive LIbrary
Des Plaines, Illinois

Published by Heinemann Interactive Library
an imprint of Reed Educational & Professional Publishing,
1350 East Touhy Avenue, Suite 240 West,
Des Plaines, IL 60018

Designed by Plum Creative
Illustrations by Oxford Illustrators
Printed in Hong Kong / China

02 01 00 99
10 9 8 7 6 5 4 3 2

Library of Congress Cataloging-in-Publication Data
Hodge, Susie, 1960–
    Ancient Roman art / Susie Hodge.
      p. cm. -- (Art in history)
    Includes bibliographical references and index.
    Summary: Examines the art of ancient Rome, including painting, mosaic, sculpture, and architecture.
    ISBN 1-57572-552-5 (lib. bdg.)
    1. Art. Roman--Juvenile literature. [1. Art, Roman. 2. Art, Ancient.] I. Title. II. Series: Hodge, Susie, 1960– Art in history.
N5760.H63   1997
709'.37--dc21
                            97–20673
                                CIP
                                AC

Acknowledgments
The author and publishers are grateful to the following for permission to reproduce copyright photographs:
AKG photo, E.Lessing pp.11 (right), 13, 28, Vatican Museums p.4; Ancient Art & Architecture Collection Ltd, R.Sheridan p.10 (left); The Bridgeman Art Library, pp.14–15, Giraudon p.19, Metropolitan Museum of Art, New York p.7, Museo Archaeologico Nazionale, Naples pp.6, 11 (left), Museo & Gallerie Nazionali di Capodimonte, Naples p.10 (right), Museum of Antiquities, Newcastle upon Tyne p.9; Corbis, R.Ergenbright p.25, R.Nowitz p.27, R.Vanni p.26, A Woolfitt p.20; C.M.Dixon pp17, 18, 24; Giraudon pp.22–23, Lauros pp.5, 12, 21, Mermet p.8; Michael Holford p.29

Cover photograph reproduced with permission of Bridgeman Art Library.

Special thanks to Paul Flux and Jane Shuter for their comments in the preparation of this book.

Every effort to contact copyright holders of any material reproduced in this book. Any omissions will be rectified in subsequent printings if notice is given to the publisher.

Cover picture: Wall painting from the Villa of Mysteries, Pompeii, mid 1st century B.C., height 5 ft, fresco.
Roman people who could afford to, paid artists to paint the walls in their homes. During the 1st century B.C., a style of wall painting developed that became known as the Second Style. Artists painted pictures that were so lifelike they looked real. In this villa just outside Pompeii, the mistress of the house asked the artist to paint a Roman story of a religion that we no longer know anything about. So the paintings have given the villa its name, the Villa of Mysteries. The artist has painted life-size, lifelike people against a brilliant red background. This is one of the most well-known examples of this style of painting, famous because of the outstanding skill of the artist.

Words in bold, **like this**, are explained in the glossary on page 31.

CONTENTS

WHAT WAS ROMAN ART?

Near the River Tiber in Italy, several small villages on seven hills grew to become the city of Rome. By 509 B.C. Rome was a **republic**. Gradually its power grew until it became a vast **empire**. By 100 A.D., Rome ruled over most of the then known world.

Adopting traditions

The Romans took over many countries, including Carthage (in North Africa), Gaul (which stretched from Italy to the Netherlands), Greece, Egypt, and Britain. They adopted the traditions that appealed to them, such as the countries' religion or art. Romans ruled, organized, and taxed the people of these countries, often mixing the best of Rome with the best of other cultures.

Many people from Rome's captive countries were employed by the Romans. Greek and Egyptian artists, for example, used their own methods to produce art for the Romans.

*Augustus, Prima Porta near Rome, about 19 B.C., 7 ft, **marble**.*

*This statue of the first Roman emperor, Augustus, (31 B.C.–14 A.D.) is by a Greek sculptor. The Romans admired the dignity of Greek **portraits** in statue form. They wanted their emperor shown as a commanding, godlike person. The back of this statue was unfinished because Roman statues stood against walls.*

Lifelike details

So the Romans took on other traditions, but added their own likes and dislikes. They admired the beauty and perfection of Greek art but they preferred lifelike details that showed people's oddities and characters.

Powerful achievements

The Romans employed artists and workmen throughout their empire to produce impressive art and to build great roads and buildings. Art and **architecture** were used to honor the gods, to celebrate events, or to proclaim someone's power. They were not just for decoration, although that was important, too. It is a sign of Roman power that their style remained similar in different lands. The Romans have had an enormous influence on art and architecture ever since.

The Triumphal Arch Of Tiberius, southern France, about 30 A.D., height 60 ft, stone.

Arches to proclaim victories were set up all over the Roman Empire. These and other buildings were designed with different sized arches and columns to make them look more interesting.

MATERIALS AND METHODS

Who became an artist?

Architects (master builders and designers) were usually educated people of the middle class. They created some of the most grand monuments in the history of **architecture**. Other artists (all called craftsmen) were usually poorer **citizens**. They worked in small workshops with a few **apprentices** and one or two slaves. Many Greek artists set up workshops so Roman artists could learn from them. Most paintings or statues were commissioned, or ordered, by wealthy citizens. Artists rarely signed their work, because they were only doing a job. Artists were not thought to be special.

*Bust of Emperor Vespasian, about 75 A.D., **marble**.*

*A bust is a statue of the head and shoulders. Roman artists made a **portrait** of anyone who could afford to pay them. They did not try to make portraits perfect, but enjoyed showing a person's characteristics. Even though he was the emperor, this bust shows Vespasian's wrinkled skin, large nose, and serious expression. Statues of emperors were put up all over the **empire** as a reminder that the Romans were in control.*

What materials did they work with?

Brushes were made from twigs, wood, lengths of reeds or rushes. They were sometimes bound with hair. Shaped wood and ivory sticks were used for drawing and writing. They were called styluses. Many wall paintings were made with paint mixed with egg yolk, called tempera. Some were in encaustic. This is where colors are mixed with wax and burned into the surface with hot irons. Most were painted in **fresco**.

For tempera and encaustic, the walls had to be smooth. They were prepared with a coating of cement, **plaster** and marble dust. This was polished before it was painted. For frescoes, walls were coated with plaster. The paint was then applied while the plaster was still wet. Most statues were polished and then painted in clear colors.

Garden of Livia, Prima Porta, near Rome, about 50–40 B.C., height 5 ft, fresco.

This is one of many wall paintings discovered in a Roman house. It is filled with fruit trees, flowers, and birds. Bluish colors help to show distance and space, brighter colors seem close up, and shadows make some objects stand out.

SIGNS AND SYMBOLS

Many of our words and alphabet letters come from Latin, the common language of the Roman **Empire**. Having one common language meant that people from different countries could communicate with each other.

Most Roman **citizens** were encouraged to learn to read. In large cities like Rome and Alexandria, there were many bookshops, libraries, and publishers.

How books were made

Books were usually scrolls (long sheets, rolled up) made out of papyrus, an Egyptian reed. The reed was cut into long narrow strips, soaked and pressed together, beaten with a mallet, left to dry, and finally polished smooth with a stone. Each book had to be written out by hand. Someone read the book to several scribes who copied the book down. Each scribe made a copy on the papyrus using reed pens. The Latin words were written in columns. Some of the scribes were artists, too, so many books were beautifully illustrated.

Virgil and the Muses, end of 2nd century to early 3rd century A.D., mosaic.

This mosaic shows the famous poet Virgil sitting between two muses. Muses are goddesses who inspire writers and artists. Virgil holds a papyrus scroll of his greatest poem, The Aeneid.

Roman letters

Scribes and stonemasons painted or carved inscriptions (words) on their monuments and statues. Two main kinds of letters were used: square capital letters for formal inscriptions and sloping italic letters for informal purposes, such as letter writing. Each letter was made of a geometric shape such as a square, triangle, or circle. At first, letters in stone were carved to one thickness. Later the sides were made to vary from thick to thin. This gave the same effect as the square-tipped brushes the stonemasons used to paint the letters on the stone first.

Inscription from Milecastle, on Hadrian's Wall, Britain, 122–125 A.D., stone.

A castle was built every mile along Hadrian's Wall on the border between England and Scotland. This inscription records the building of one Milecastle by the Second Legion Augusta. The letters were chiseled by hand and the little check-like marks at the ends of letters are where the stonemasons rested their chisels as they carved. We use similar check shapes on some printed letters even now and call them serifs.

PAINTING TECHNIQUES

The Romans loved to have paintings in their homes and public buildings. They did not have wallpaper, so artists painted pictures directly on to the walls and ceilings. Floors were also painted. Small panel paintings on wood were hung on walls or displayed on stands called easels. These were sold from artists' workshops.

Fresco was used for most walls. This made the colors brighter and helped the painting to last. When the background was dry, details were added. All kinds of scenes were painted, such as gods and heroes, hunting and farming, landscapes, and animals. **Portraits** of the owners of houses were popular, too.

Trick pictures

Four different styles of Roman wall painting developed.

First style Walls were painted to look as if they were made of **marble**, or were copies of Greek styles of decoration.

House of Citharist, Stabiae, Naples, 1st century B.C., fresco.

This house had a series of frescoes running around it that were similar to those in Greek homes. Some houses had marbled effects painted on the walls.

Second style Realistic looking scenes tricked the eye. They looked like views through windows.

Room from the Villa of Mysteries, Pompeii, mid 1st century B.C., height 5 ft, fresco.

The background of brilliant red and the black dividing lines do not look realistic, but the life-sized figures certainly do. 29 figures and numerous scenes run continuously around the room, making it appear larger than it really is.

Third style Less realistic, but often delicate looking pictures.

Fourth style A combination of the second and third styles.

Spring, Maiden Gathering Flowers, Stabiae, Naples, about 15 B.C.–60 A.D., fresco.

This might be a goddess, or simply the lady of the house, picking flowers as if in a dance. Gracefully draped in a colored robe, this is painted in a gentle, fresh style.

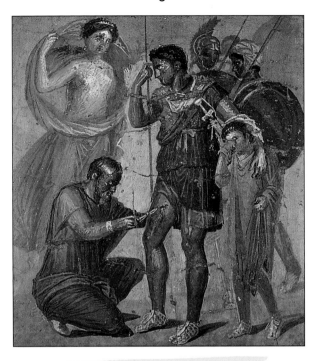

Healing of the Wounded Aeneas by Iapyx, Pompeii, 1st century A.D., fresco.

This painting shows the story of Doctor Iapyx healing the hero Aeneas. The goddess Venus heals him, too, although the humans cannot see her.

Paint palette

Paints were made from ground rocks, powdered plants, or animal dyes. Red and yellow came from ochre (a clay-like substance), white from chalk, green from green soil, blue from a mixture of glass and copper, black from soot, and purple from a special seashell. The **pigments** were mixed with lime, milk, egg, or **gum** to make a paste.

STORYTELLING PICTURES

As well as inscriptions and books, the Romans used paintings and raised carvings known as reliefs, to tell stories of their war victories. The Greeks had done this, too. But where the Greeks used **symbolism** to tell their stories, the Romans showed the real, sometimes gory, details.

Ancient customs

These narrative, or story-telling, pictures had been a custom hundreds of years before in China. During those times, kings ordered monuments announcing their victories in war. Later these monuments developed into complete picture-stories. Wealthy Romans liked the idea of proclaiming Roman triumphs for all to see. Artists were employed to paint or carve heroic stories.

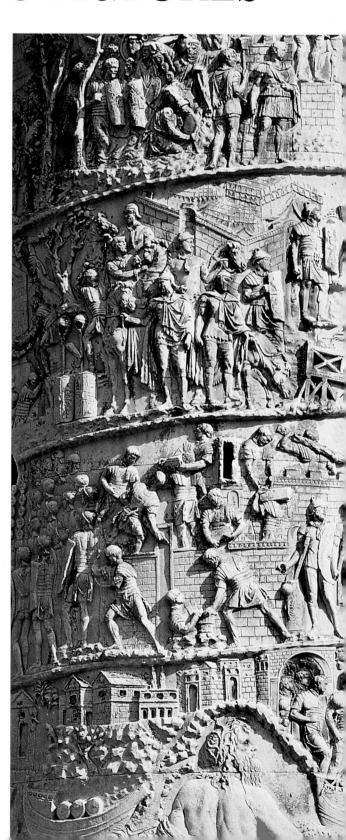

*Trajan's Column, Rome, 113 A.D., height 125 ft, **marble**.*

The emperor Trajan ordered a huge column to be made to show the story of his wars. Like in a comic strip, Trajan appears in a continuous, lively story that spirals around the column.

The Great Hunt, Piazza Armerina, Sicily, early 4th century A.D., mosaic.

Artists from Africa made this large floor mosaic. The most important part of the picture is the figures. Their hair and clothes, and the animals' fur and feathers are detailed, although the trees and rocks are small and decorative. Trying to make the picture look realistic was not the aim. The picture was to tell a story and look attractive.

Art for everyone

Like advertising today, these great works of art convinced and persuaded people. They proudly announced victories. At the same time, they told people that the Roman **Empire** was the greatest.

Most narrative art was about battles. Some stories of gods, goddesses, heroes, and legends were also painted and carved. Roman art was meant to be seen and enjoyed by many. Artists worked hard at making it easily understood.

Public and private art

Works of art that showed the Roman Empire and its emperors as strong and generous were put in public places for all to see. Story-telling pictures were painted inside private houses. These were done by interior decorators, not major artists.

MOSAIC ART

Mosaics became popular from the 1st century A.D. A mosaic is a picture or pattern made from small pieces of colored glass or stone. They decorated walls and floors.

How mosaics were made

Artists drew a design of the mosaic they were going to make. Then they spread wet **plaster** over a small area of the floor or wall and smoothed it down. They quickly pressed the pieces of stone into the plaster while it was still damp, following their design.

At first, patterns in black and white were the most common. They remained fashionable around Rome. But farther afield, by the 2nd century A.D., more colorful mosaics became popular. Companies of artists designed mosaics in their workshops. People chose a design, then the mosaic artist came to the house with the chosen plan and the stones already cut. Several artists would work on one mosaic.

Orpheus Playing to the Animals, Antioch in Turkey, about 2nd century A.D., mosaic.

The Roman god, Orpheus, plays a lyre, charming the animals around him. Shadows and highlights make the picture look three-dimensional. See how contented all the animals look as they listen to the music!

Make your own mosaic

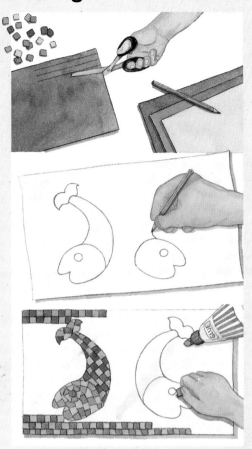

Materials:

several sheets of colored paper or thin posterboard

scissors

glue

large sheets of white paper or thin posterboard

pencil

1. Cut the colored paper or posterboard into small squares.

2. Draw the outline of your mosaic on a large sheet of white paper or posterboard.

3. Stick the colored squares in place on your outline, leaving a tiny space between each of your squares, so that the mosaic looks realistic.

Bird and Bunch of Grapes, Badajoz in Spain, about 350 B.C., mosaic.

Brightly colored pieces of stone called tesserae have turned this wall into a beautifully decorated area. It is meant to be a pattern, rather than realistic, although you can see clearly what it represents. Mosaics in this style were used to decorate fountains, too.

ART FOR THE GODS

The Romans adopted religions as well as styles of art from the countries they took over. They gave their adopted gods and goddesses different names. For example, Aphrodite was the Greek goddess of love and beauty. The Romans called her Venus. Until Christianity was adopted, the Romans did not believe in worshiping just one god. Because of this, it made sense to allow the people in the countries they took over to keep their old gods.

The Romans did not believe that their paintings, statues, and reliefs of gods showed real events. They were made to remind people about the gods they were worshiping and to please the gods themselves. Some pictures showed people performing rituals for the gods. Some showed wondrous stories of supernatural strength and power. Some, like the statue of Augustus on page 4, showed that the gods protected the good and the great.

Mars and Venus, from the House of Lucrezio Frontone, Pompeii, 1st century A.D. **fresco**.

According to Roman religion, Mars, the god of war, loved Venus. Roman artists often painted the two together, sometimes showing them as ordinary humans. On the left, Mars wears military dress, with helmet, lance, and breastplate. Venus, sitting in front of him, wears a long tunic and light cloak, like a wealthy Roman woman. Cupid, the god of love, stands in the center, while other citizens look on.

Household gods

The Romans worshiped thousands of gods and spirits. The most important gods and goddesses were Jupiter, Neptune, Venus, and Minerva. They were well known to Roman **citizens** throughout the **empire** because all kinds of art had been made in these gods' honor. Apart from the main gods, every house had its own shrine called a Lararium. At this shrine the people worshiped the household gods, called Lares, every day. The Lararium was often carved and decorated, with small statuettes and painted friezes (decorations that run in a band).

Venus Marina, Pompeii, before 79 A.D., fresco.

Venus, the goddess of love, is in a magical seashell being towed by Cupid and some dolphins. She did not have to look realistic because she is a symbol. The artist has made her up from his imagination. This fresco and many others were painted on the walls of houses in Pompeii and Herculaneum. The walls were covered in volcanic ash when the volcano Vesuvius erupted in 79 A.D. This preserved the frescoes.

ROMAN SCULPTURE

Sculptors and stonemasons were hired to make statues for public buildings and private villas. Statues were originally brightly painted, but the paint has now worn off. Gods, goddesses, animals, and **portraits** of real people were common subjects.

Titus, Rome, about 80 A.D., ***marble***.

This portrait of the Emperor Titus was part of a full-length sculpture that showed him commanding everyone to look up to him by looking stern and mighty. It was made to show his power and importance. Statues of emperors were put up all over the empire as a reminder that the Romans were in control.

Commemorative statues

There was great demand for **commemorative** statues. They were placed in public squares, halls, or temples. Some were put on top of commemorative columns. Most were of emperors and other important people, symbolizing victory and power. Roman sculptors had learned from Greek sculptors how to show draped material over what appears to be a living body. They enjoyed the challenge of creating realistic looking fabric hanging in folds on the body, as well as realistic looking faces. Along with statues in armor, these portrait statues were grand and lifelike reminders of their rulers to the **citizens** of the Roman Empire.

Scenes from everyday life

Roman artists also carved details from daily life. Often these were made for sarcophagi (stone coffins) or tombstones to tell stories of a dead person's life. These relief carvings show scenes like mothers bathing their babies, people working or relaxing, or wedding ceremonies. They all seem natural looking and relaxed. They also give us a wonderful insight into everyday Roman life.

Roman butcher, 2nd century B.C., stone frieze.

This relief probably decorated a Roman butcher's shop. The butcher is chopping meat on a block. You can see other kinds of meat hanging on hooks above. Notice the little details that the artist has included, such as the pulley and rope, and the folds of the butcher's toga.

CLASSICAL STYLE

The term "classical art" usually refers to the art of the ancient Greeks and Romans. The classical style is carefully designed and balanced.

Borrowing ideas

The Romans copied the Greeks, but the Greeks originally learned from the Egyptians. They borrowed Egyptian ideas, but were able to improve such crafts as **marble** carving and **bronze casting** because they had better tools. This allowed them to create more realistic images than the Egyptians. The Romans then borrowed and adapted the Greeks' ideas.

Marcus Aurelius, 161–80 A.D., height 11 ft, bronze.

This is the only large-scale Roman bronze statue that survived to the present day. After the Romans converted to Christianity, bronze statues of non-Christian emperors or gods were melted down. This statue was mistakenly believed to be of a Christian emperor, so it was saved. The emperor's pose is lifelike. The weight of the rider and horse is carried on three legs which was a difficult effect to produce.

Detailed descriptions

In the 1st century A.D., a scribe called Pliny wrote an encyclopedia of natural sciences and arts. He described many Roman artists and their methods, such as the casting of bronze. Pliny's book was useful to artists centuries later. They learned skills that might otherwise have been forgotten.

Skillful sculptors

Sculptors became highly skilled, drawing many sketches, then making clay, wax, or **plaster** maquettes (small test models of the sculpture). **Marble**, bronze, wood, and wax were used for most statues and reliefs. The lost-wax method of casting was used often. First a model was made in wax. Then a clay mold was made around it. When baked, the wax melted away and the clay became the mold for the bronze to be poured into. The clay mold was later broken open to reveal the solid bronze statue.

The Goddess Hecate, Yugoslavia, about 1st century A.D., marble.

The Romans loved art and color. Most statues were brightly painted originally, but the color has now worn away. Sculptors produced many beautifully draped female forms like this. They concentrated on proportion and balance, and made every feature stand out clearly.

SCULPTURE FOR ALL

At first it was customary to carry wax images of ancestors in Roman funeral processions. Romans believed that this preserved the dead person's soul. Later, when the **empire** stretched to distant lands, Romans burned incense in front of busts, (head and shoulder statues) of their emperors, treating them like gods. Sacrifices were also brought to shrines for their gods. This proved the people's faith and devotion.

Statues everywhere

Romans put sculpture on display everywhere. Many sculptures were **portraits**. Others, like Trajan's Column on page 12, were reliefs that told a story, often of Roman triumph. All these sculptures were a form of reporting and **propaganda**. They reminded people of the power of the Roman Empire.

Most sculptures were more than just decoration. Sea creatures, like dolphins which symbolized the god Cupid, were built into fountains. Gods, goddesses, heroes, and animals appeared in town squares (called forums), temples, public buildings, and houses. Often forums displayed statues of the town's patron god.

*Claudius, 51–54 A.D., life-size, **marble**.*

When new, this sculpture would have been full length, brightly painted, and polished. Roman sculptors produced lifelike statues of their emperors. Many later emperors thought of themselves as gods. They told their people that they should be worshiped as gods. Whether or not people really believed they were gods, it was safer to act as if they did!

Families

The family was important to the Romans. Statues and paintings of family members, alive and dead, were made and displayed in their homes and gardens. Statues of the Lares, gods of the household, were also shown.

Detail from The Ara Pacis Augustae, 13–19 B.C., height 5 ft, marble relief.

The Ara Pacis Augustae was a large marble altar given by Emperor Augustus. It was dedicated to peace and to the people. The stories carved into the walls are a mix of history and legend. This is the emperor Augustus and his family. The people in the background are carved faintly, while those in the foreground are clearer.

ROMAN BUILDINGS

Early Roman towns had no particular plan. But as the **empire** grew and became more organized, the Romans began to arrange their towns. They needed public baths, meeting places, government buildings, and temples for worship. A style for towns was developed. The most important public buildings were placed around a central forum. The rest of the town spread out from the forum in a grid pattern.

Columns and arches

The Romans used five types of column for important buildings. They are adapted from Greek columns. Roman architects and engineers also worked out how to build **domes**, **vaults**, and arches.

Arches cross wider gaps and support more weight than the straight beams of wood or stone that had been used previously. So, with arches, Roman buildings grew larger and stronger.

*The Baths of Caracalla, Rome, 212 A.D., originally stone, glass, concrete, and **marble**.*

There were public baths throughout the Roman Empire, but the ones in Rome were particularly magnificently decorated. It is hard to imagine now, but in Roman times, this ruin was a richly decorated and popular building (big enough for 1600 people). There were hot, warm, and cold baths, as well as exercise and lecture rooms, libraries, and snack bars. You can still see the remains of the vaulted ceilings. Vaulted ceilings were arches overlapping at right angles.

A strong invention

The Greeks had used stone for building, but the Romans developed concrete. They made it with lime, sand, and water, plus small stones, pieces of rock, or pottery. Because concrete could be spread smoothly before drying, architects were able to develop new curved shapes on wooden frames.

By the 2nd century B.C., Roman builders added powdered volcanic stone (called pumice) to make a concrete that was strong and waterproof. Architects coated the outside of concrete buildings with polished brick or marble.

The Pont du Gard, Agrippa, in France, 19 B.C., height 12 ft, stone.

This is another great achievement in Roman building. It is an aqueduct. It was 24 miles long and was built to channel water to the town of Nîmes in France. Three tiers of arches cross the River Gard. Many similar aqueducts were built throughout the empire to bring fresh water to towns.

BIG BUILDINGS

New building methods meant that Roman buildings and monuments were strong. Roman architects were the first to build high-rise apartment buildings!

The Pantheon, Rome, originally 25 B.C., completed 125 A.D., Agrippa and Hadrian, concrete, brick, and **marble**.

This new form of temple was originally planned by Emperor Augustus's lieutenant, Agrippa. It was eventually completed when Hadrian was emperor. It is a masterpiece of both art and engineering. The domed ceiling is surprisingly large. It is 140 ft across. It was meant to represent the curve of heaven. In the center a hole, 28 ft across, provides light and air.

Tools and equipment

The Romans developed ways of producing bricks in standard sizes and shapes. They were baked in very hot ovens called kilns to make them stronger than sun-dried bricks. Clay tiles and gutters were baked in a similar way. Bricks set in cement were often used in arches, **domes** and **vaults**.

Various tools, such as the groma, were used to estimate straight lines. Wooden scaffolding was used to support builders as they worked and to keep blocks of stone in place. The Romans even used wooden cranes to help lift and position heavy objects. The cranes were driven by treadmills and were linked to pulleys.

Huge arena

One of the most famous Roman buildings is the huge arena in Rome known as the Colosseum. Arches, vaults, and concrete meant that architects could design and build this spectacular sight. It was covered in gleaming white marble, with statues on every arch.

The Colosseum was used for shows that featured gladiators or animals fighting, or for the execution of enemies of the **empire**. During the intermissions, spectators were sprinkled with perfume to mask the smell of blood from the arena.

The Colosseum, Rome, 72–80 A.D., height 160 ft, stone and concrete.

The Colosseum seated 50,000. Beneath the ground, a huge network of chambers housed the animals and people before their performances. The arena could even be flooded for staged naval battles. The foundations were 40 ft deep. Columns were added all around the auditorium, where the people watching stood or sat. There even might have been a movable canopy to shade the open area from the sun.

EARLY CHRISTIAN ART

Christians, unlike most other religious groups, worshiped only one God. This meant that they refused to worship the emperor. So, at first the Romans tried to stamp out Christianity. But the number of Christians grew. In 312 A.D. the new emperor, Constantine, became a Christian and made Christianity legal. Art began to change.

Secret art

For many years, Christians had to worship in secret. They met in catacombs (underground passageways). They designed secret symbols and included them in paintings of Bible stories on the walls of the catacombs.

The Miracle of the Loaves and Fishes, Ravenna, Italy, about 520 A.D., mosaic.

When Christianity was accepted, artists began using Bible stories as subjects. This shows the New Testament story when Jesus fed 5,000 people with five loaves and two fish. The Romans tried to make Christianity acceptable by using familiar images from other religions. Jesus, in this picture, is copied from the old Roman god, Apollo.

A curious mixture

We know that Roman artists could make true-to-life images, but the picture opposite looks stiff. There are shadows on the ground and in the folds of cloth, but other lifelike details were no longer necessary. It was more important to use recognizable symbols than to produce realistic art.

Church design

Christians modeled their churches on basilicas (large, rectangular assembly halls). These became the basic design for Christian churches everywhere. Statues in new churches were discouraged. But because many people could not read or write, paintings and reliefs taught them about their new religion.

The end of classical art

It was not just Roman art that was changing. The **empire** had grown too big and its emperors could not control it. The Roman army began to retreat and left the countries around the edges of the empire. Gradually the empire crumbled and other people took over, bringing new ideas with them.

*Symbol of Christianity, Lullingstone Villa, Kent, England, late 4th century A.D., wall painting, **fresco**.*

This painting decorates a wall inside a Roman villa that was first built in the 1st century A.D. It is one of the first symbols that Christians used as a mark of their beliefs. Even the colors had a special significance.

TIME LINE

B.C.

753	Legendary date of when Rome was founded.
509	Last king expelled from Rome, republic formed.
500	Romans begin to take over neighboring parts of Italy.
265	Rome controls the whole of Italy.
204	Rome invades Africa.
202	Rome seizes parts of Spain.
179	First stone bridge over the River Tiber.
140	Romans conquer Greece and most of Spain.
59–51	Conquest of Gaul.
55	Invasion of Britain.
50–40	Odyssey landscapes painted. Also, wall paintings in the Villa of Mysteries, Pompeii.
30	Conquest of Egypt.
27	Augustus becomes the first emperor (beginning of the Roman Empire).
25	Agrippa, Augustus's lieutenant and son-in-law, designs a temple in Rome.
19	The Pont du Gard aqueduct designed and built by Agrippa.
13–9	The Ara Pacis Augustae altar is built (commissioned by Emperor Augustus).
about 5 A.D.	Birth of Jesus in Bethlehem.
14	Tiberius becomes emperor.
79	Pliny the elder (author who described artists and their methods) dies while investigating a volcanic eruption.
30	The Triumphal Arch of Tiberius is built. Many monuments, reliefs and inscriptions are produced to tell stories of victories.
41–54	Britain is conquered. Busts and portraits of the emperors are worshiped as gods.
54–68	Emperor Nero rules and tries to get rid of all Christians.
72–80	The Colosseum is designed and built.
79–81	Titus is emperor. The volcano Vesuvius erupts (79), destroying the towns of Herculaneum and Pompeii on the west coast of Italy.
101	Trajan becomes emperor and commissions his column.
117–138	Hadrian is emperor. Builds a wall separating England and Scotland. The Pantheon is built on the site of Agrippa's earlier temple in Rome.
138–312	Many emperors rule. Plague, famine and wars interrupt peace and power.
312–37	Emperor Constantine rules. He becomes Christian and stops persecution of Christians. Christian art is no longer secret art.
337–64	Many other emperors rule.
410	Roman Empire is reduced. Unrest continues.

GLOSSARY

apprentices These are people learning a trade or craft by working with a skilled worker.

architecture This is the art of designing and constructing buildings

bronze This is a hard-wearing brownish gold metal made of a mixture of copper and tin.

casting This is producing a sculpture using a mold

citizens inhabitants of a city who had many legal, political, and other privileges were called citizens. Not everyone was a citizen. Slaves, for example, were non-citizens and had no privileges.

commemorative This term means ways of keeping things in people's memories. Memorials and celebrations are commemorative.

composition This is the layout or arrangement of art.

dome A vault rising up from a round base, usually shaped like one half of a hollow ball is a dome.

empire The land ruled by an emperor, usually made up of more than one country, is called an empire.

fresco This is a painting made on a damp, freshly plastered wall.

gum The sticky substance from plants, used to hold pigments together, is called gum.

marble This is a hard rock that can be polished to a high shine. It comes in many patterns and colors.

pigment The colored powder made from plants, minerals, or animals and mixed with various liquids to make paint is called pigment.

plaster This is a fine white powder made from a rock called gypsum. It is mixed with water, then left to dry.

portrait Pictures or sculptures of a particular person or people is known as a portrait.

propaganda Publicity that spreads ideas or information that will influence people is called propaganda.

republic This is a country without a hereditary ruler.

symbolism This is where pictures use symbols for meanings, rather than real, factual images.

vault A curved ceiling made by arches is a vault. A barrel, or tunnel, vault is a group of arches together. A groin vault is two barrel vaults crossing at right angles.

MORE BOOKS TO READ

Corbishley, Mike. *What Do We Know About the Romans?* New York: Peter Bedrick, 1992.

Macdonald, Fiona. *First Facts About the Ancient Romans.* New York: Peter Bedrick, 1996.

INDEX

Numbers in plain type (24) refer to the text. Numbers in bold type (**28**) refer to an illustration.